孔子学院总部/
国家汉办汉语国际推广成都基地规划教材

走 进 天 府 系 列 教 材【成都印象】

Let's Watch Sichuan Opera

西 南 财 经 大 学
汉语国际推广成都基地   著

西南财经大学出版社
中国·成都

西 南 财 经 大 学
汉语国际推广成都基地　著

总策划　涂文涛

策 划
李永强

主 编
梁　婷　白巧燕

编 者
《成都印象·游成都》　胡倩琳
《成都印象·居成都》　郑　莹
《成都印象·吃川菜》　谢　娟　王　新
《成都印象·品川茶》　肖　静
《成都印象·饮川酒》　谢　娟
《成都印象·看川剧》　郑　莹
《成都印象·绣蜀绣》　谢　娟
《成都印象·梦三国之蜀国》　蒋林益　胡佩迦
《成都印象·悟道教》　沙　莎　吕　彦　陈　茉
《成都印象·练武术》　邓　帆　刘　亚

审 订　冯卫东

英文翻译
Alexander Demmelhuber

Introduction

Let's Watch Sichuan Opera is one part of the "Impressions of Chengdu" textbook series, which is promoted by the Chengdu Base of Confucius Institute Headquarters and published by the Southwestern University of Finance and Economics. This book contains 5 units, which are designed on the basis of the Confucius Institute Headquarters'/Hanban's "International Curriculum for Chinese Language Education" (hereinafter referred to as "Curriculum"), as can be seen, for example, on vocabulary and language points used, and ensures that this textbook is held to scientific, systematic and rigorous standards. The main premise of this book is Sichuan opera as it can be seen in Chengdu, including, but not limited to, a short introduction of Sichuan opera, the famous "Legend of the White Snake", Sichuan opera in Jinjiang Theater, face changing and artistic features. This book not only introduces Sichuan opera, but also takes vocabulary and language points into consideration, in order to help Chinese language students enjoy Sichuan opera in Chengdu.

This book is mainly composed of vocabulary and grammar items that can be found in the Curriculum for levels 3 to 6, with some everyday Chinese expressions mixed in. We hope that this book will help deepen the cultural knowledge of Chinese students possessing a middle to high level of Chinese, and also serve to improve their Chinese proficiency.

Hopefully, you will enjoy *Let's Watch Sichuan Opera* and we are looking forward to any criticism or suggestions you might have. Hanban gave us much help and support during editing of this book and we would like to take this opportunity to express our gratitude.

前言

　　《看川剧》是西南财经大学汉语国际推广成都基地推出的《成都印象》系列教材之一。全书共 5 课,以孔子学院总部/国家汉办的《国际汉语教学通用课程大纲》为基本编写依据,涉及大纲中的大量词汇、语言点等指标,以保证教材的科学性、系统性和严谨性。本书以在成都看川剧为线索,包括川剧简介、川剧名篇《白蛇传》、去锦江剧院看川剧、变脸、川剧的艺术特色等内容,力求在介绍川剧的同时,兼顾词汇和语言点,为外国汉语学习者在成都看川剧提供语言和信息的支持。本书语言材料以大纲中的 4-5 级词汇和语法项目为主,加入了一些生活中的常用汉语,希望能够扩宽中高级水平汉语学习者的文化视野,全面提升汉语水平。

　　希望您能喜欢《看川剧》这本教材,也希望您对本书提出批评和建议。本书的编写得到了国家汉办的大力支持和帮助,在此一并表示感谢。

目 录

第一课
Lesson 1
〔 川剧简介 〕
〔 A Short Introduction of Sichuan Opera 〕
01 - 05

第二课
Lesson 2
〔 川剧名篇《白蛇传》〕
〔 A Masterpiece of Sichuan Opera:
Legend of the White Snake 〕
06 - 17

第三课
Lesson 3
〔 去锦江剧院看川剧 〕
〔 Sichuan Opera in Jinjiang Theater 〕
18 - 27

第四课
Lesson 4

〔变脸〕
〔Face-Changing〕

28 - 35

第五课
Lesson 5

〔川剧的艺术特点〕
〔Artistic Characteristics of Sichuan Opera〕

36 - 48

〔参考文献〕
〔References〕

49

第一课 【川剧简介】
Lesson 1 【A Short Introduction of Sichuan Opera】

① 风 趣　　fēngqù
② 浓 厚　　nónghòu
③ 气 息　　qìxī
④ 群 众　　qúnzhòng
⑤ 冠　　　guàn
⑥ 欣 赏　　xīnshǎng
⑦ 地 道　　dìdào
⑧ 遭 遇　　zāoyù
⑨ 考 验　　kǎoyàn
⑩ 改 良　　gǎiliáng
⑪ 任重道远　rènzhòng dàoyuǎn
⑫ 瞒　　　mán
⑬ 亲 切　　qīnqiè
⑭ 非物质文化遗产保护名录
　　fēi wùzhì wénhuà
　　yíchǎn bǎohù mínglù

　　川剧是流行于四川、重庆、云南、贵州等部分地区的戏剧形式，它有着悠久的文化和历史。川剧以表演为中心，反映了西南地区人民的日常生活、思想情感和审美情趣，也体现了人们的聪明才智和艺术追求。

　　川剧是四川文化的特色之一，其中的特技如"变脸""吐火"等世界闻名。川剧用四川话演唱，语言风趣幽默、生动活泼，具有很浓厚的生活气息，是广大人民群众喜闻乐见的艺术形式。

　　成都是著名的戏剧之乡，早在唐代就有"蜀戏冠天下"的说法，在成都可以欣赏到地道的川剧。但是川剧在现代社会中也遭遇了不小的考验，川剧的改良和发展任重道远。2006年，川剧被列入国家第一批非物质文化遗产保护名录。

文小西：
　　你平时看川剧吗？

大 萌：
　　不瞒你说，我以前也没有看过，第一次看川剧也是和外国朋友一起去的。

文小西：
　　看了之后，你觉得自己喜欢川剧吗？

大萌：
　　喜欢，挺有意思的，跟你们看歌剧一样，而且是用四川话唱的，我觉得很亲切。你想一起去看场川剧吗？

文小西：
　　用四川话唱，那我怎么听得懂呢？

大萌：

你不是要学四川话吗？可以感受一下。要是遇到听不懂的地方，我可以给你解释解释。

文小西：

就这么说定了。叫上一华一起吧。

大萌：

没问题。

Sichuan opera is a popular form of drama in Sichuan, Chongqing, Yunnan, Guizhou and other parts and regions. It has a long history and culture. Sichuan opera focuses on performance and reflects not only the daily life, emotions and aesthetic conceptions of the people living in Southwest China, but also their intelligence and wisdom as well as their artistic pursuits.

Sichuan opera is one of the characteristics of Sichuanese culture and uses world-famous dramatic arts such as "face-changing" and "fire-spitting". Sichuan opera is performed in the Sichuanese dialect, and features humorous and vivid language as well as a strong feel of everyday life. It is a popular art form among a vast number of people.

Chengdu is a famous home of drama. As early as the Tang Dynasty, there already was the saying, "Sichuan is the best place for drama in the world". In Chengdu, you can enjoy pure Sichuan opera. However, in modern society, Sichuan opera has faced many trials, and it has had a long way to go for improvement and development. In 2006, Sichuan opera was included in the first batch of the national list of intangible cultural heritage.

Wen Xiaoxi: Do you usually watch Sichuan opera?

Da Meng: To be frank, I've never watched it before. When I watched it for the first time, I also did so with some friends from abroad.

Wen Xiaoxi: After you've watched it, do you think you like it?

Da Meng: I do. It was quite fascinating; it was like watching Western opera with you people, but the songs were in Sichuanese, which really touched me. Do you want to watch together?

Wen Xiaoxi: If it's sung in Sichuanese, how are we even going to understand anything?

Da Meng: Didn't you say you wanted to study Sichuanese? Just give it a try. If there's anything you don't understand, I'll explain it to you.

Wen Xiaoxi: Then it's settled. Let's ask Yihua to come with us.

Da Meng: All right!

词 语

气 息 qìxī flavor	群 众 qúnzhòng the masses	瞒 mán conceal from

fēng qù 风 趣	humor, wit	zāo yù 遭 遇	meet with; encounter
nóng hòu 浓 厚	dense; thick; strong; pronounced	kǎo yàn 考 验	test; put to the test; trial; ordeal
dì dào 地 道	authentic; genuine; pure;typical	gǎi liáng 改 良	improve
xīn shǎng 欣 赏	appreciate; enjoy	pī 批	batch; lot; group
guàn 冠	top; the best	qīn qiè 亲 切	close; intimate; dear; familiar

| rèn zhòng dào yuǎn
任 重 道 远 | a heavy load and a long road; to bear heavy responsibilities for a long time |
| fēi wù zhì wén huà yí chǎn
非 物 质 文 化 遗 产
bǎo hù míng lù
保 护 名 录 | Intangible cultural heritage list |

语 言 点

一、补语

1. 可能补语
   听得懂、听不懂
2. 结果补语
   说定了

三、插入语

不瞒你说

二、ABAB式重叠

解释解释

第二课 【川剧名篇《白蛇传》】
Lesson 2 【A Masterpiece of Sichuan Opera: "Legend of the White Snake"】

《白蛇传》是中国四大民间爱情传说之一，讲述了一个修炼成人的蛇与人之间的曲折爱情故事。一条小白蛇被一个年轻的牧童救了，在峨眉山下修

炼千年拥有了人形，之后来到杭州寻找前世的救命恩人。白蛇取名白素贞，在途中认识了青蛇小青，她和白素贞一样，拥有人形。她们在西湖边遇到了白蛇前世的救命恩人许仙。白素贞使用法术让天下雨，与许仙一起坐船，两人一见钟情。许仙把伞借给了她们，并在分别的时候，商量好了还伞的时间和地点。

后来两人坠入爱河并结为夫妇，一起经营一家中医药铺。白素贞美丽大方、聪明能干，许仙精通医术。他们免费为穷人治病，受到当地老百姓的称赞，生活过得很幸福，但镇江金山寺的僧人法海一直阻挠他们的爱情。他告诉许仙他的妻子是蛇精，

① 民间　mínjiān
② 传说　chuánshuō
③ 修炼　xiūliàn
④ 蛇精　shéjīng
⑤ 曲折　qūzhé
⑥ 牧童　mùtóng
⑦ 前世　qiánshì
⑧ 救命恩人　jiùmìng ēnrén
⑨ 法术　fǎshù
⑩ 一见钟情　yíjiàn zhōngqíng
⑪ 商量　shāng liang
⑫ 坠入爱河　zhuìrù àihé
⑬ 夫妇　fūfù
⑭ 经营　jīng yíng
⑮ 药铺　yàopù
⑯ 大方　dà fang
⑰ 能干　nénggàn
⑱ 精通　jīngtōng
⑲ 免费　miǎnfèi
⑳ 老百姓　lǎobǎixing
㉑ 称赞　chēngzàn
㉒ 僧人　sēngrén
㉓ 阻挠　zǔnáo
㉔ 端午节　Duānwǔjié

㉕	千辛万苦	qiānxīn-wànkǔ
㉖	骗	piàn
㉗	哀 求	āi qiú
㉘	放	fàng
㉙	除 非	chúfēi
㉚	投 降	tóuxiáng
㉛	否 则	fǒuzé
㉜	无 奈	wúnài
㉝	闪 电	shǎndiàn
㉞	划	huá
㉟	漫	màn
㊱	灾 害	zāihài
㊲	洪 水	hóngshuǐ
㊳	伤 害	shānghài
㊴	趁 机	chènjī
㊵	相 遇	xiāngyù
㊶	坦 白	tǎnbái
㊷	身 份	shēnfèn
㊸	接 受	jiēshòu
㊹	满 月	mǎnyuè
㊺	无能为力	wúnéng-wéilì
㊻	关	guān
㊼	感 慨	gǎnkǎi
㊽	诧 异	chàyì
㊾	恐 怖	kǒngbù
㊿	冒 险	màoxiǎn
51	怀 孕	huáiyùn
52	善 良	shànliáng
53	撒 谎	sāhuǎng

让他在端午节劝白素贞喝酒。白素贞喝了酒变成了白蛇，许仙差点儿被吓死。白素贞经历千辛万苦，终于把许仙救活。

后来，许仙被法海骗到金山寺，无论白素贞怎么哀求，法海都不放人。他说除非白素贞投降，否则他不会把许仙交出来。白素贞无奈使用法术下起了大雨，一道闪电划过天空，雨水漫过金山寺造成了灾害，洪水伤害了无数的生命。许仙趁机逃出金山寺，与白素贞、小青在断桥相遇。

白素贞向许仙坦白了自己蛇精的身份，许仙感受到白素贞的爱接受了她。后来，白素贞生下了一个儿子。孩子满月时，白素贞被法海带走，许仙和小青无能为力。白素贞被关在雷峰塔下。后来小青练成了武功，救出了白素贞。

文小西：

这个故事太曲折了，感慨他们之间的爱情。但是有的地方我不太明白，甚至挺诧异的，为什么人可以和蛇在一起呢？太恐怖了！

大萌：

别怕，这只是个传说。白蛇变成人，有了人的情感，她为了爱情冒险，甚至怀孕生子，我们都觉得她是个善良的人，不是蛇。

可是她为什么撒谎呢？为什么不肯早点说出事实？

大 萌：

一方面可能是害怕吓着许仙，另一方面怕他不能接受自己是蛇精的身份，以致撒了谎吧。

江一华：

我去杭州旅行的时候也听说过这个浪漫的爱情故事。

大 萌：

这是一个家喻户晓的神话爱情故事，电视里经常播放的电视剧《新白娘子传奇》，讲的就是《白蛇传》，不过和川剧的故事情节有一些不同，比如白蛇练功的地方在青城山，最后结局也不太一样：电视剧中白蛇的儿子长大考中状元，到雷峰塔前探望母亲，并将母亲救出，一家人团圆。

江一华：

杭州西湖边现在还有断桥、雷峰塔等景点，都是《白蛇传》里的吗？

大 萌：

是的，历史上先有这些景点，后来才有了《白蛇传》的传说。《白蛇传》被列入"第一批国家级非物质文化遗产"。白蛇不再邪恶，成为纯洁爱情的象征。

54 肯　　　　kěn
55 以 致　　yǐzhì
56 浪 漫　　làngmàn
57 家喻户晓　jiāyù hùxiǎo
58 情 节　　qíngjié
59 结 局　　jiéjú
60 中状元　　zhòng zhuàngyuan
61 探 望　　tànwàng
62 救　　　　jiù
63 团 圆　　tuányuán
64 景 点　　jǐngdiǎn
65 邪 恶　　xié è
66 纯 洁　　chúnjié
67 象 征　　xiàngzhēng

68 根深蒂固　gēnshēn dìgù
69 启 发　qǐfā

> 文小西：
> 这个故事打破了一些根深蒂固的思想，对我启发挺大的。

The Legend of the White Snake is one of China's Four Great Folktales and tells a love story with many twists between a man and a snake that has turned human after practicing austerity. A little white snake was rescued by a young shepherd boy. To express its gratitude to him, the snake went to Mount Emei to practice austerity for a thousand years in order to turn human and afterwards went to Hangzhou to search for its savior from a previous life. The white snake adopted the name "Bai Suzhen", met on its way the green snake called Xiaoqing, who was another snake that had turned human, and together they finally met Bai Suzhen's savior Xu Xian at the West Lake in Hangzhou. Bai Suzhen cast a spell to make it rain and took a boat together with Xu Xian where the two fell in love at first sight. Xu Xian lent his umbrella to the two ladies and, before parting, told them when and where to return his umbrella.

Later, they fell head over heels in love with each other and married; they also ran a Chinese herbal medicine shop. Bai Suzhen was beautiful and generous, smart and capable, while Xu Xian was proficient in medicine. They treated the poor for free and were held in high regards by the locals. They led a happy life. But Fahai, a monk of Jinshan Temple in Zhenjiang, was trying to obstruct their love. He told Xu Xian that his wife was a snake spirit and made him persuade Bai Suzhen to drink alcohol during the Dragon Boat Festival. After Bai Suzhen drank the wine, she turned into a white snake, which almost scared Xu Xian to death. Bai Suzhen went through innumerable hardships and finally saved Xu Xian's life.

Later on, Xu Xian was fooled by Fahai and led to Jinshan Temple. No matter how much Bai Suzhen pleaded, Fahai did not let him go. He said that he would not hand over Xu Xian unless Bai Suzhen surrendered. Bai Suzhen felt helpless and cast a spell to cause heavy rain with lightning striking across the sky. The rain water built up and flooded Jinshan Temple, causing a calamity which cost countless lives. Xu Xian took this chance to escape from Jinshan Temple and happened to meet Bai Suzhen and Xiaoqing on the Broken Bridge.

Bai Suzhen admitted to Xu Xian that she was a snake spirit, which made him feel Bai Suzhen's love toward him. Later on, Bai Suzhen gave birth to a boy. When the child was one month old, Bai Suzhen was taken away by Fahai and Xu Xian and Xiaoqing were powerless. Bai Suzhen was locked up under the Leifeng Pagoda. Xiaoqing practiced martial arts to rescue Bai Suzhen.

Wen Xiaoxi: This plot takes an awful lot of turns. I'm deeply moved by the love of those two. There are some points I don't really get or leave me really flabbergasted. How can people and snakes be together? That's terrifying!

Da Meng: Don't be afraid. It's only a legend. The white snake turned human and because she felt the love of another person, she braved danger and even bore a child, all in the name of love. All of us think that she's a kind woman and not a snake.

Wen Xiaoxi: Why did she lie, though? Why was she not willing to tell the truth earlier?

Da Meng: On one hand, she might have been afraid of scaring Xu Xian; on the other hand, she was afraid that he wouldn't accept her as a snake spirit. So that's what probably made her lie.

Jiang Yihua: When I went to Hangzhou, I also heard of this romantic love story.

Da Meng: Everybody knows this mythical love story in China. The *Madame White Snake* TV series is often shown on TV, which also tells the Legend of the White Snake, but it differs in some regards from the story as it is told in Sichuan opera. For example, the white snake practiced martial arts on Mount Qingcheng and the ending is also not the same: In the TV series, after the white snake's son grows up, he comes first in the highest imperial examination and becomes Number One Scholar. It is he who goes to Leifeng Pagoda to look for his mother and rescue her to reunite the family.

Jiang Yihuang: Are the Broken Bridge at West Lake in Hangzhou and the Leifeng Pagoda the same as in the *Legend of the White Snake*?

Da Meng: They are. These places existed before the Legend of the White Snake. The *Legend of the White Snake* was included in the "first batch of the national intangible cultural heritage". The white snake, rather than a symbol of evil, became a symbol of pure love.

Wen Xiaoxi: This story has changed some deep-rooted thoughts of mine and has made me look at things in a new light.

词 语

 shǎndiàn
闪 电 lightning

 kǒngbù
恐 怖 terrifying; frightening

 xié' è
邪 恶 sinister; evil; wicked; vicious

mín jiān 民 间	among the people; popular; folk
xiū liàn 修 炼	practice austerity
mù tóng 牧 童	shepherd boy
jiù mìng ēn rén 救 命 恩 人	savior; life saver
yí jiàn zhōngqíng 一 见 钟 情	fall in love at first sight
zhuì rù ài hé 坠 入 爱 河	fall into the river of love; fall head over heels in love

chuán shuō 传 说	legend; folk tale
shé jīng 蛇 精	snake spirit; snake demon
qián jīng 前 世	previous incarnation; previous life
fǎ shù 法 术	magic; magic arts
shāng liang 商 量	consult; discuss; talk over
fū fù 夫 妇	husband and wife

dà fang 大 方	generous
jīng tōng 精 通	proficient in; have a good command of
lǎo bǎi xìng 老 百 姓	ordinary people; the "person in the street"
gēn shēn dì gù 根 深 蒂 固	deep-rooted
jīng yíng 经 营	manage; operate; run
zǔ náo 阻 挠	thwart; obstruct
qiān xīn wàn kǔ 千 辛 万 苦	innumerable trials and tribulations; untold hardships
āi qiú 哀 求	entreat; implore; plead
chú fēi 除 非	(with "否则") (not) unless

néng gàn 能 干	capable; competent
miǎn fèi 免 费	free (of charge)
chēng zàn 称 赞	praise; commend
qǐ fā 启 发	enlighten; stimulate
sēng rén 僧 人	(Buddhist) monk
duān wǔ jié 端 午 节	Dragon Boat Festival
piàn 骗	deceive; fool; swindle; cheat
fàng 放	let go; set free; release
tóu xiáng 投 降	surrender; capitulate

fǒu zé 否 则	if not; otherwise; else
huá 划	strike; slash; cut; scratch
zāi hài 灾 害	calamity; disaster
shāng hài 伤 害	injure; harm
xiāng yù 相 遇	meet; encounter; come across
shēn fèn 身 份	identity
mǎn yuè 满 月	baby's completion of its first month of life
guān 关	shut in; lock up; confine
gǎn kǎi 感 慨	deeply moved
mào xiǎn 冒 险	take risks/chances

wú nài 无 奈	helpless; have no choice
màn 漫	overflow; brim over; flood
hóng shuǐ 洪 水	flood
chèn jī 趁 机	take advantage of the occasion; seize the chance
tǎn bái 坦 白	confess; admit
jiē shòu 接 受	accept
wú néng wéi lì 无 能 为 力	powerless; helpless; incapable of action
qū zhé 曲 折	complicated; winding; twisting
chà yì 诧 异	surprised; astonished
huái yùn 怀 孕	be pregnant

shàn liáng 善 良	good and honest; kindhearted
kěn 肯	willing to do sth
làng màn 浪 漫	romantic
qíng jié 情 节	plot
zhòng zhuàng yuan 中 状 元	score the highest in the imperial examination system
jiù 救	rescue; save
jǐng diǎn 景 点	scenic spot
xiàng zhēng 象 征	symbol; stand for

sā huǎng 撒 谎	tell a lie; lie
yǐ zhì 以 致	(usu. referring to bad results) consequently; as a result
jiā yù hù xiǎo 家 喻 户 晓	known to every household; widely known; known to all
jié jú 结 局	conclusion; ending
tàn wàng 探 望	look around
tuán yuán 团 圆	(of family members) reunite; have a reunion
chún jié 纯 洁	pure; clean and honest
yào pù 药 铺	herbal medicine shop

语言点

一、补语

1. 程度补语
   生活得很满足

2. 结果补语
   打破

3. 趋向补语
   交出来、救出、说出

二、句型

1. 复句
   ① 因果复句　因为……所以……，以致
   ② 条件复句　除非……否则……

2. 把字句

3. 被字句

思 考

本课讲述了川剧名篇《白蛇传》的故事，这是个传奇的民间爱情故事，白蛇和许仙产生了感情并结婚生子。你怎么看白蛇的身份？你觉得这部戏剧表达了怎样的思想情感？

第三课 【去锦江剧院看川剧】
Lesson 3 【Sichuan Opera in Jinjiang Theater】

大萌：

今天我们去锦江剧院看场川剧吧。

江一华：

锦江剧院在哪里？

大萌：

锦江剧院在成都市锦江区华兴正街 54 号，临近春熙路，在王府井商场背后。它位置优越，交通便利，既处于繁华的闹市区，又有一份成都特有的味道。

文小西：

好啊，今天是什么剧目？

大萌：

锦江剧场每天都在演的《芙蓉国粹·川剧传奇变脸》。

江一华：

这部川剧主要讲了什么内容？

① 优 越　yōuyuè
② 便 利　biànlì
③ 繁 华　fánhuá
④ 味 道　wèidào

⑤剧 目　jùmù
⑥字 幕　zìmù
⑦融 合　rónghé
⑧领 略　lǐnglüè
⑨台上一分钟，台下十年功
　　tái shàng yì fēnzhōng,
　　tái xià shí nián gōng
⑩轻 松　qīngsōng
⑪吃 苦　chīkǔ

大 萌：

它讲述了两位明末清初的川剧艺人曲折的爱情故事。它并不是传统的川剧剧目，是现代艺术家融合了川剧的各种艺术特色创作出来的。现场除了有英语字幕以外，还有日语和韩语的字幕。在这一部川剧中你们不仅可以看到川剧变脸、吐火、变服装、木偶戏、滚灯等各种特技，而且可以欣赏到一些传统川剧的片段，领略川剧的基本功。

文 小西：

川剧的基本功有哪些？

大 萌：

川剧讲究"唱、念、做、打"。"唱"指的是歌唱，"念"指音乐性的念白，"做"是指舞蹈化的身体动作，"打"指武术。许多川剧演员从小就开始练习戏剧的基本功，我们说"台上一分钟，台下十年功"，演员在台上的演出看起来轻松自然，其实在日常训练时是吃了很多苦的。

文 小西：

想起来了，我看过一部讲中国戏剧的电影《霸王别姬》，戏剧演员为了把戏演好从小便开始接受非常严格的训练。

大萌：

戏剧演员熟练掌握了基本功和固定程序之后，也可以有一些自我创造。"师傅领进门，修行在个人"，相同的角色不同的演员可以演出不同的特点，同一个演员演同一个角色，可能每天都会不一样。

江一华：

艺术也是一种个人化的体验吧。那我们快去感受一下。我们怎么去锦江剧场呢？

大萌：

坐地铁 4 号线，从西南财大站到市二医院，出了地铁站走路 10 分钟就到了，当然我们也可以骑共享单车过去。

（到了锦江剧院）

大萌：

这就是川剧艺术中心，是在清末的剧社和茶园的基础上修复建成的。中间是锦江剧院，右边是川剧艺术博物馆，旁边是悦来茶楼，左边是川菜馆盘飧市。"锦江"和"盘飧市"的名字都是来自杜甫的诗句。

文小西：

杜甫是唐代的大诗人，杜甫草堂离我们学校也很近。

⑫师傅领进门，修行在个人
　shīfu lǐngjìnmén,
　xiūxíng zàigèrén
⑬共享　　gòngxiǎng
⑭修复　　xiūfù
⑮陈列　　chénliè

⑯文 物　　wénwù
⑰物美价廉　wùměi-jiàlián
⑱络绎不绝　luòyì bùjué
⑲浓 厚　　nónghòu
⑳独 特　　dútè

大萌：

对，川剧艺术博物馆可以免费参观，里面陈列着一些跟川剧有关的文物，介绍川剧的小知识。我们买了票之后还可以去悦来茶楼免费喝盖碗茶。四川人平时喜欢去茶馆，在茶馆人们可以聊天、打麻将、谈生意，茶馆消费不高，物美价廉，来来往往的茶客络绎不绝，生活气息浓厚。

江一华：

一边喝茶，一边看着川剧舞台上演着别人的故事，也是四川人民独特的生活方式吧。

大萌：

是啊，平时生活忙碌，难得来一趟茶馆。川剧表演马上就要开始了，我们快走吧。

Da Meng: Today we're going to Jinjiang Theater to watch Sichuan opera.

Jiang Yihua: Where is Jinjiang Theater?

Da Meng: Jinjiang Theater is at 54 Huaxing Street, Jinjiang District, near Chunxi Road, behind Wangfujing mall. Its location is excellent and easily reachable with public transport. It is both located in the bustling downtown area and gives off vibes typical of Chengdu.

Wen Xiaoxi: All right! So what's today's program?

Da Meng: Jinjiang Theater shows a performance of *The essence of Chengdu: Sichuan opera's legendary face-changing.*

Jiang Yihua: What is this piece mainly about?

Da Meng: It is about a love story with many twists between to Sichuan opera artists set in late Ming and early Qing (around the middle of the 17th century). It is not a traditional piece of Sichuan opera. Contemporary artists created this program by mixing together various artistic characteristics of Sichuan opera. In addition to English subtitles, this piece can also be seen with Japanese and Korean subtitles. In such a piece of Sichuan opera you can not only see face-changing, fire-spitting, costume-changing, puppetry, rolling light and many more routines, you can also appreciate some traditional Sichuan opera and have a taste of Sichuan opera's fundamental techniques.

Wen Xiaoxi: What are these fundamental techniques?

Da Meng: Sichuan opera focuses on "singing, reading, doing, and fighting", where "singing" refers to song singing, "reading" to the spoken parts, "doing" to dancing moves and "fighting" to martial arts. Many actors start practicing these fundamental techniques of drama from an early age. There is a saying, "Ten years of practice for one minute on the stage", which describes an actor's performance as natural and effortless, while they, in fact, faced a lot of hardships during their daily training.

Wen Xiaoxi: I just remembered that I once saw a movie called *Farewell my Concubine* about Chinese opera. In order to deliver a convincing performance, the actors started their extremely rigorous training form an early age.

Da Meng: Actors who have mastered the fundamental techniques and the fixed procedures are allowed some creativity of their own. There is a saying that is applicable here, "A master teaches the trade, but the apprentice's skill is self-made". Different actors may deliver different performances for the same role. Even if the actor and their role are the same, their performance may still not be the same every day.

Jiang Yihua: Art is also a kind of personal experience, so let's go and experience it for ourselves. How do we get to Jinjiang Theater?

Da Meng: We will take Metro Line 4 from the SWUFE station to Chengdu Second People's Hospital. From there, it will take us ten minutes by foot to arrive. We can also ride a shared bike to get there, of course.

(After arrival at the Jinjiang Theater)

Da Meng: This is the Sichuan Opera Arts Center, which was renovated and built out of a theater society and a tea garden from the final years of the Qing Dynasty. In the middle is the Jinjiang Theater, and on the right is the Sichuan Opera Art Museum, next to it is the Yuelai Teahouse, and on the left is the Sichuan restaurant Pansunshi. The names "Jinjiang" and "Pansunshi" both stem from Du Fu's poems.

Wen Xiaoxi: Du Fu was a great poet of the Tang Dynasty. The Du Fu Thatched Cottage is also close to our school.

Da Meng: Right. Visiting the Sichuan Opera Art Museum is free. There, a number of cultural relics related to Sichuan opera are on display for us to learn more about Sichuan opera. After buying the tickets, we can also go to Yuelai Teahouse to have a cup of tea for free. The Sichuanese like going to teahouses, where they can chat, play mahjong and do business. Teahouses aren't expensive. Their services are cheap but good, and attract a continuous flow of customers. They are bustling with life.

Jiang Yihua: Having tea while watching actors perform on stage is also a way of life unique to the Sichuanese, I'd say.

Da Meng: It is! Life is usually very busy, and people rarely have the chance to go to the teahouse. The show is about to begin. Let's get going.

词语

 xiūfù
repair; restore;
renovate

 wèidào
taste; flavor;
feeling; experience

 fánhuá
flourishing;
bustling

yōu yuè 优 越	superior; advantageous; favourable	biàn lì 便 利	convenient; easy; facilitate
jù mù 剧 目	repertoire; program; list of plays or operas	lǐng lüè 领 略	have a taste of; appreciate
zì mù 字 幕	subtitle	chī kǔ 吃 苦	bear hardships
gòng xiǎng 共 享	share	qīng sōng 轻 松	relaxed; effortless
chén liè 陈 列	display; exhibit	wén wù 文 物	cultural relic
wù měi jià lián 物 美 价 廉	good quality and cheap; a bargain	luò yì bù jué 络 绎 不 绝	continuously; in an endless stream
nóng hòu 浓 厚	thick; strong; pronounced	dú tè 独 特	unique; distinct

tái shàng yì fēn zhōng tái xià shí nián gōng 台 上 一 分 钟，台 下 十 年 功。	Ten years of practice for one minute on the stage.
shī fu lǐng jìn mén xiū xíng zài gè rén 师 傅 领 进 门，修 行 在 个 人。	A master teaches the trade, but the apprentice's skill is self-made.

语言点

一、连谓短语
　　去锦江剧院看川剧

二、复句

　　1. 递进复句
　　　 不仅……而且

　　2. 因果复句
　　　 由于……，因此……

　　3. 假设复句
　　　 倘若……也

　　4. 并列复句
　　　 一边……一边

三、介词
　　除了……（以外）……还……

思 考

本课中，三人一起去锦江剧院看川剧，聊到了川剧的基本功、川剧艺术中心等内容。你看过川剧吗？你心中理想的川剧是什么样子？

第四课 【变脸】
Lesson 4 【Face-Changing】

文小西：

刚才这场川剧表演非常精彩，故事情节感动得我热泪盈眶。

江一华：

我正纳闷儿呢，你怎么看得泪汪汪的。

文小西：

这两位主角纯真的爱情太难能可贵了。

江一华：

舞台很华丽，演员的表演更是锦上添花。变脸、吐火的功夫真是太不可思议了。大萌，你可以给我们介绍一下川剧里的这些功夫吗？

大 萌：

变脸是川剧中演员在创造角色时使用的一种表演手法，它用各种脸谱的变换来表现剧中人物的性格和内心思想情感的变化。它把难以体会的情绪和心理状态变成了可见可感的脸谱。

① 热泪盈眶　　rèlèi yíngkuàng
② 纳闷儿　　　nà mènr
③ 泪汪汪　　　lèi wāngwāng
④ 难能可贵　　nánnéng-kěguì
⑤ 锦上添花　　jǐnshàng-tiānhuā
⑥ 不可思议　　bùkě-sīyì
⑦ 教　训　　　jiàoxùn
⑧ 板　凳　　　bǎndèng
⑨ 翻跟头　　　fān gēn tou
⑩ 趣　味　　　qùwèi
⑪ 任　凭　　　rènpíng
⑫ 无理取闹　　wúlǐ-qǔnào
⑬ 心甘情愿　　xīngān-qíngyuàn
⑭ 折　腾　　　zhēteng

江一华：

除了变脸，滚灯在川剧中也挺有特点的。

大 萌：

对，滚灯最早出现在川剧《皮金滚灯》中。剧中的男主角皮金很喜欢打麻将，而且常常输了钱被老婆教训。老婆惩罚他把油灯顶在头上，他顶着灯跳舞、钻板凳、翻跟头，甚至跳到高凳上把油灯吹灭，情节趣味十足。

⑮反 抗　　fǎnkàng
⑯举足轻重　jǔzú-qīngzhòng
⑰与日俱增　yǔrì-jùzēng
⑱㞎耳朵　　pā ěrduo
⑲理所当然　lǐsuǒ dāngrán
⑳知足常乐　zhīzú chánglè
㉑谅解　　　liàngjiě
㉒扯　　　　chě
㉓气功　　　qìgōng
㉔油彩　　　yóucǎi
㉕预先　　　yùxiān

文小西：

剧中皮金没有大男子主义，他被老婆惩罚，完全不生气呢。

大 萌：

剧中的皮金夫妻是典型的四川小夫妻形象，丈夫温柔，妻子泼辣。任凭妻子无理取闹，皮金心甘情愿被老婆折腾，也不反抗。

文小西：

四川女人性格热情开朗外向，像她们经常吃的辣椒一样，因而被叫作"辣妹子"。

大 萌：

四川女人不仅在家里的地位举足轻重，而且能在社会生活中体现自身价值，女性的社会地位与日俱增。

江一华:

据说在四川怕老婆的男人被称为"炒耳朵"。

大 萌:

确实是这样。与其说四川男人怕老婆，不如说他们爱老婆。四川女人精明能干，家人也都很尊重她们的意见，四川男人在家做家务也是理所当然。四川人讲究知足常乐，这些日常生活里的乐趣也体现了人性的温暖。

江一华:

不如我们一边涮火锅一边再聊聊川剧中的艺术吧。

㉖绸　子　chóu zi
㉗重　叠　chóngdié
㉘特　定　tèdìng
㉙丝　线　sī xiàn
㉚掩　护　yǎnhù
㉛白　酒　báijiǔ
㉜煤　油　méiyóu
㉝导火线　dǎohuǒ xiàn

　　川剧常见的变脸方法有四种，分别是"抹脸""吹脸""扯脸"和"气功"。"抹脸"是指演员将化妆油彩预先涂在脸的某一特定部位上，需要时用手一抹，脸上就变成了其他颜色。"吹脸"是指演员将粉末状的化妆品放在酒杯或舞台上的小盒子里，演员贴近盒子，闭眼，用嘴一吹，脸色就变了。最常见的是"扯脸"，即演员把画在绸子上的多张脸谱重叠在一起，贴在脸上，每一张脸谱有一根特定的丝线系在衣服上，演员表演的时候，在舞蹈动作的帮助下把重叠在脸上的脸谱一张一张地扯下来，表现出人物的喜怒哀乐。
　　变脸体现了川剧的精华，其他的特技如吐火、滚灯也各有特色。吐火虽然有一定的危险性，但是戏剧表现力强。演员嘴里含着煤油或高浓度的白酒，然后深吸一口气，一口吐在前面的导火线上，形成一团巨大的火焰。在眼前的火焰还没熄灭之前演员绝对不能吸气，不然会被火焰烧伤。要练习吐火的特技，需要先反复练习吐水，直到把水吐成雾状才算合格。

Wen Xiaoxi: The performance just now was brilliant! The plot moved me to tears.

Jian Yihua: I'm surprised you got all teary-eyed.

Wen Xiaoxi: The two protagonists' mutual love was simply remarkable!

Jiang Yihua: The stage was beautiful, and the actors' performance was the icing on the cake. Face-changing, fire-spitting and so on were really incredible. Da Meng, could you tell us more about these acts?

Da Meng: Face-changing is a kind of performance technique used by Sichuan opera actors to create roles. They use various masks to express change of thoughts and emotions of characters in a play. This technique makes the audience be able to understand and feel emotions and mental states that would otherwise be difficult to convey.

Jiang Yihua: Apart from face-changing, rolling light is also quite characteristic of Sichuan opera.

Da Meng: Correct. Rolling light made its first appearance in the Sichuan opera piece *Pijin Rolls the Light*. The main lead Pijin loves playing mahjong. He also often loses money and is lectured by his wife. She punishes him by putting an oil lamp onto his head. Balancing the oil lamp, he dances, crawls under stools, turns somersaults and even jumps onto a high chair to make the oil lamp go out. The plot is really fun.

Wen Xiaoxi: Pijin is no alpha male at all. He gets punished by his wife, but doesn't get angry at all.

Da Meng: Pijin and his wife portray the typical image of the Sichuanese husband and wife relationship, where the husband is gentle and the wife is fierce and unreasonable. No matter how unreasonable his wife acts, Pijin is perfectly happy to be tormented by his wife and doesn't resist.

Wen Xiaoxi: Sichuanese women are passionate and out-going, just like the chili peppers they eat. That's why they are also called "spicy girls".

Da Meng: Sichuanese women not only play a critical role at home, they are also able to hold their own in society and steadily climb the social ladder.

Jiang Yihua: It is said that Sichuanese men who fear their wives are called "henpecked".

Da Meng: This is indeed the case. Rather than saying, "they fear their wives", it'd be better to say, "they love their wives". Sichuanese women are bright and capable, and their family members deeply respect their opinions. Their husbands consider it as their natural duty to do the chores at home. The Sichuanese know that contentment brings happiness. These joys of everyday life reflect the kindness and warmth in their relationships.

Jiang Yihua: How about enjoying some hotpot while we chat about the art of Sichuan opera?

There are four common ways of face-changing, namely "face-dragging", "blowing dust", "pulling-down masks" and "qigong"(controlled breathing).

"Face-dragging" refers to an actor applying greasepaint to a particular part of their face in advance. If needed, they can simply drag the greasepaint and their face will change color. "Blowing dust" refers to an actor placing powdered cosmetics in a small box on a goblet or the stage. The actor stands close to the box, closes their eyes, blows into the box and voila, and their face changes color. "Pulling-down masks" is the most common technique. An actor takes several pieces of silk on top of each other, where each piece of silk has a mask painted on it, and puts them on their face. Each mask has a designated thread of silk on the actor's clothing. During the performance and facilitated by dancing moves, the actor may pull off the overlapped masks one by one, expressing the characters' emotions. Face-changing reflects the essence of Sichuan opera. Other acts such as fire-spitting and rolling light are also special in their own rights. Although fire-spitting is dangerous to a certain degree, it is a powerful form of expression. Inside the actor's mouth is kerosene or highly concentrated baijiu, which, after taking a deep breath, the actor spits on a fuse, causing a huge flame. The actor cannot take a breath before the flame has gone out, otherwise they will be burned. In order to practice fire-spitting, actors have to repeatedly practice spitting water until they manage to form the water into mist.

词语

báijiǔ
Chinese white spirit

dǎohuǒxiàn
fuse

rè lèi yíng kuàng 热泪盈眶	eyes brimming with tears; moved to tears	nà mènr 纳闷儿	feel puzzled; be perplexed; wonder
lèi wāng wāng 泪汪汪	tearful (of a vulnerable person or animal)	nán néng kě guì 难能可贵	rare and precious; valuable; remarkable
jǐn shàng tiān huā 锦上添花	make what is good still better; put the icing on the cake	bù kě sī yì 不可思议	inconceivable; unimaginable; unfathomable
chě 扯	pull; tear	qì gōng 气功	qigong (a system of deep breathing exercises)
yóu cǎi 油彩	greasepaint	yù xiān 预先	in advance; beforehand
chóu zi 绸子	silk fabric	chóng dié 重叠	overlap; one on top of another

tè dìng 特 定	special; specific; designated
yǎn hù 掩 护	screen; shield; cover
jiào xùn 教 训	chide sb; lecture sb; give sb a talking to
fān gēn tou 翻 跟 头	turn a somersault
wú lǐ qǔ nào 无 理 取 闹	be unreasonably troublesome; act up; make trouble without reason
xīn gān qíng yuàn 心 甘 情 愿	perfectly happy to do; most willing to do; delighted to do
fǎn kàng 反 抗	resist
yǔ rì jù zēng 与 日 俱 增	increase steadily; grow with each passing day
lǐ suǒ dāng rán 理 所 当 然	as a matter of course; as it should be by rights
liàng jiě 谅 解	understand; make allowance for

sī xiàn 丝 线	silk thread
méi yóu 煤 油	kerosene
bǎn dèng 板 凳	wooden bench or stool
qù wèi 趣 味	fun; interest; delight
rèn píng 任 凭	(conjunction) no matter (how, what, etc.); even if; even though
zhē teng 折 腾	torment; do sth. over and over again; play crazy
jǔ zú qīng zhòng 举 足 轻 重	play a crucial role; influential
pā ěr duo 炮 耳 朵	henpecked; be under one's wife's thumb
zhī zú cháng lè 知 足 常 乐	contentment brings happiness; satisfied with what one has; count one's blessings
shuàn huǒ guō 涮 火 锅	cook in a hotpot

语言点

一、插入语
据说

二、复句

1. 承接复句
……于是……

2. 因果复句
……，因而……

3. 转折复句
虽然……但是……

4. 选择复句
与其……不如

5. 转折复句
……不然的话……

三、成语的使用

思考

本课介绍了川剧中的特技——变脸、吐火和滚灯的具体方法，并谈论了四川特有的"辣妹子"和"㞎耳朵"现象。你可以用自己的语言说说变脸和吐火吗？你们国家的戏剧有没有使用特技？如果有的话，请具体介绍一下。

第五课 【川剧的艺术特点】
Lesson 5 【Artistic Characteristics of Sichuan Opera】

【一】

文 小西：

川剧中的特技真是不可思议！变脸演出时全场轰动，现场高潮不断。

江 一华：

我觉得看《皮金滚灯》的时候特别热闹，剧情幽默，音乐也恰到好处。演奏的乐器是中国传统的乐器吧？

大 萌：

是的，川剧里使用的乐器都是四川民间乐器。开场的时候气氛很活跃。以前川剧开始的时候就这样吸引观众，现在依然保留着这样的传统。

文 小西：

演员的衣服很漂亮，色彩鲜艳，这有什么讲究吗？

①	不可思议	bùkě sīyì
②	轰动	hōngdòng
③	掀	xiān
④	高潮	gāocháo
⑤	恰到好处	qiàdào hǎochù
⑥	演奏	yǎnzòu
⑦	乐器	yuèqì
⑧	气氛	qìfēn
⑨	活跃	huóyuè
⑩	依然	yīrán
⑪	保留	bǎoliú
⑫	讲究	jiǎngjiu
⑬	行头	xíngtou
⑭	靴	xuē
⑮	胡须	húxū
⑯	崇高	chónggāo
⑰	华丽	huálì
⑱	皇帝	huángdì
⑲	打扮	dǎbàn
⑳	鲜明	xiānmíng
㉑	脸谱	liǎnpǔ
㉒	激烈	jīliè
㉓	豪迈	háomài
㉔	残忍	cánrěn
㉕	正直	zhèngzhí
㉖	粗鲁	cūlǔ
㉗	沉着	chénzhuó
㉘	坚韧	jiānrèn

㉙门　帘　ménlián
㉚对　应　duìyìng
㉛墨　水　mòshuǐ
㉜呈　现　chéngxiàn
㉝竹　竿　zhúgān
㉞联　想　liánxiǎng
㉟归根到底　guīgēn-dàodǐ
㊱风土人情　fēngtǔ rénqíng
㊲飞禽走兽　fēiqín zǒushòu
㊳桨　　jiǎng
㊴平　静　píngjìng
㊵波　涛　bōtāo
㊶汹　涌　xiōngyǒng
㊷仔　细　zǐxì
㊸负　担　fùdān
㊹遮　挡　zhēdǎng
㊺集　中　jízhōng
㊻忽　略　hūlüè
㊼成　本　chéngběn
㊽屏　幕　píngmù
㊾耗　费　hàofèi
㊿资　源　zīyuán

大萌：

古代的戏服称为"行头"，分为服装、头帽、靴鞋和口条（嘴巴附近的装饰，如胡须）。不同的衣服颜色可以体现人物的身份、地位和年龄。如地位崇高的人衣服华丽，黄色是古时候皇帝的颜色。通过看演员的打扮，就可以知道他的身份。

江一华：

演员化妆用的颜色很鲜明，是同样的意思吗？

大萌：

对，川剧用脸谱的不同来表现人物的性格和情绪。一般来说，红色脸谱代表人物性格激烈豪迈、忠诚英勇；黄色表示勇敢或残忍的性格；黑色既可以代表正直、严肃的人物，也可代表威风、粗鲁的人物；紫色表示沉着、坚韧的性格；青色是魔鬼的形象；等等。每次上场之前演员都会花大量的时间化妆。

文小西：

不同颜色的脸谱挺好看的，有装饰的作用。舞台上布置的东西也非常有中国特色。

大 萌：

川剧在一个舞台上表演，就要用一些物品来表示所处的环境。比如挂着门帘，摆着桌椅板凳，桌子上有酒，说明这是一个饭馆儿。桌子上摆放着毛笔和墨水，旁边有书架，就表示这里是书房。拿一根竹竿表示钓鱼，就联想这里不仅有山、有水，还有鱼。归根到底，这个小小的舞台可以展现各种风土人情、表现各类飞禽走兽的活动，艺术表现力极其丰富。

江一华：

演员手里拿着一支桨，加上表演，就是在水里划船。这水可能是平静的河水，也可能是波涛汹涌的长江水，演员用不同的姿势和手法，加上船上人的各种表情，就把不同的水的大小表现出来了。

大 萌：

你观察得非常仔细。另外，舞台上的物品还会有一些其他的作用。比如门帘可以遮挡后台的活动，让观众的注意力只集中在演员身上，忽略其他工作人员在为下一场戏做的准备工作。

(51)门 票 ménpiào
(52)开 支 kāizhī
(53)精 心 jīngxīn
(54)策 划 cèhuà
(55)传 承 chuánchéng
(56)闭 塞 bìsè
(57)多 元 duōyuán
(58)冲 击 chōngjī
(59)众所周知 zhòngsuǒ-zhōuzhī
(60)大不了 dàbùliǎo
(61)归根到底 guīgēn-dàodǐ
(62)反 思 fǎnsī
(63)品 味 pǐnwèi
(64)急于求成 jíyú qiú chéng
(65)明 智 míngzhì
(66)迎 合 yínghé
(67)得天独厚 détiān-dúhòu
(68)优胜劣汰 yōushèng-liètài
(69)欣欣向荣 xīnxīn-xiàngróng
(70)精益求精 jīngyì-qiújīng
(71)再接再厉 zàijiē-zàilì
(72)复 兴 fùxīng

【二】

文小西：

> 这么大的舞台和剧场成本应该挺高的，灯光、屏幕、舞台、人员，会耗费不少的资源、花很多钱吧。门票能维持剧场的开支吗？

大 萌：

> 这个剧场由专门的公司经营，这个剧目也是精心策划的。

江一华：

> 来看戏的人主要是游客和外国人，好像没有本地的年轻人来看，那川剧传承也面临着一些困难吧？

大 萌：

> 是啊，这个话题说起来有点沉重，这也是现在川剧发展面临的问题，观众数量减少，市场缩小。以前相对闭塞，艺术形式比较单一，现在流行文化越来越多元，对川剧产生了不小的冲击。变脸、吐火等方法已经众所周知了。不过现在有一些外国人对川剧产生了浓厚的兴趣，甚至有外国人在学习川剧呢！

文小西：

虽然川剧在时代的发展中遭遇了一些挫折，但是也没什么大不了的，重要的是找到问题的根源，解决问题。

江一华：

归根到底，川剧面临着一个传承和创新的问题。川剧演出的剧目主要是传统的剧目，没有家喻户晓的新作，艺术的形式也需要更多的创新。川剧应该更符合年轻人的品味，才可以吸引他们来到剧场。

大萌：

急于求成也不明智，不能为了迎合年轻人的目光而丢失传统。在四川发展川剧，有着得天独厚的优势。如果想在优胜劣汰的市场竞争中保持欣欣向荣的发展形势，首先需要保留川剧的特色，在坚持传统的同时精益求精。其次还要创新，在之前的基础上再接再厉。

文小西：

据我所知，现在的川剧艺术也在尝试创新。

大 萌：

对，比如在使用中国传统乐器的同时，加入西方的乐器，使用西方音乐的唱法等。国家也很支持川剧的复兴，比如修建了川剧艺术中心，组织"川剧进校园"活动，让更多的人了解川剧、喜欢川剧。

文小西：

除了在锦江剧院，还能在哪里看到川剧呢？

大 萌：

你还可以在蜀风雅韵看川剧，在琴台路文化公园，在那儿你可以尝试化个川剧的妆。另外宽窄巷子、一些火锅店也会有川剧表演。

[|]

Wen Xiaoxi: Sichuan opera's acts are unbelievable! During face-changing the whole audience went wild! The show was exciting from beginning to end!

Jiang Yihua: I felt watching *Pijin's Light Rolling* was a lot of fun, the plot was humorous and the music just right. The instruments used in the performance were traditional Chinese instruments, right?

Da Meng: Right. The instruments used in Sichuan opera are all Sichuanese folk instruments, which make the atmosphere at the start of an opera very lively. Through this method, the Sichuan opera attracted viewers in former times, and has retained this tradition to this very day.

Wen Xiaoxi: The actors' clothes are gorgeous and colorful! Is there more to them?

Da Meng: During ancient times, these clothes were known as "paraphernalia" and consisted of costumes, headgear, boots and shoes as well as mouthpieces (adornment worn close to the mouth, for example beard pieces). Differently colored attire may reflect the identity, status and age of the characters. Characters of very high social standing, for example, wear resplendent clothing, where yellow is the color worn by ancient emperors. By watching the way the actors dress, you can tell their characters' identity.

Jiang Yihua: The actors'makeup is also brightly colored. Is the connotation the same?

Da Meng: It is. Different masks convey the characters'dispositions and emotions. Generally speaking, a red mask represents an unyielding, heroic, loyal and brave character; yellow stands for a brave or cruel disposition; black symbolizes an upright and serious-minded, or mighty and boorish character; purple indicates calm and tenacious natures; light green denotes demons, and so on. Before each performance, the actors spent a lot of time on makeup.

Wen Xiaoxi: The differently colored masks are quite the looker and fulfill a decorative function. The things arranged on stage also simply ooze Chinese culture.

Da Meng: Because Sichuan opera is performed on a stage, the use of some items is necessary to represent environments. For example, curtains, tables and chairs, with alcohol placed on the table, represent a restaurant. Brush and ink placed on a table with shelves next to it, we know that is supposed to show a study. The use of a bamboo pole represents fishing, which the audience associates with mountains, water and fish. Ultimately, the stage, albeit small, can show all kinds of local conditions and customs as well as various animals. Sichuan opera's artistic expression is extremely rich.

Jiang Yihua: If actors hold a paddle and perform accordingly, this means that they row a boat in the water. This body of water may be a calm river or the raging Yangtze River. Actors use different poses and means in addition to the different people's manner on the boat, in order to express the size of a body of water.

Da Meng: A keen observation. Also, the items on stage still fulfill some other roles. For example, curtains may cover background activities, letting the audience focus on the actors and overlook other staff members' preparation work for the next scene.

[II]

Wen Xiaoxi: The costs for running such a huge stage and a theater should be quite high. Lighting, screens, stage and staff consume a lot of resources. Are ticket sales enough to support these expenses?

Da Meng: This theater is run by a specialized company and their program is well-planned.

Jiang Yihua: It looks like that mainly tourists and people from other countries come here to watch opera and nobody from the local youth. Isn't Sichuan opera facing challenges when it comes to continuing its tradition?

Da Meng: Absolutely! This is somewhat of a heavy topic. Yes, Sichuan opera is facing these problems, the number of viewers is declining, and the market is shrinking. The entertainment market used to be quite inaccessible, and art forms were rather unified. Now, pop culture is getting increasingly diverse, inflicting a heavy blow to Sichuan opera. Face-changing, fire-spitting and so on are well-known among the locals and are nothing new. Having said that, there are some people from aboard who are taking a keen interest in Sichuan opera and some of them are even studying it!

Wen Xiaoxi: Although Sichuan opera suffered some setbacks during its history, it's no big deal. What's important is to find the root of the problem and solve it.

Jiang Yihua: Ultimately, Sichuan opera is facing a problem of inheritance and innovation, and shows mainly traditional programs. There are no well-known new pieces. The art form needs more innovation. Sichuan opera should be more in line with young people's tastes to attract them to the theater.

Da Meng: Undue haste won't produce proper results. We shouldn't sacrifice tradition to cater to young people. Sichuan opera is well-equipped to thrive in Sichuan. If Sichuan opera wants to continue to thrive in a dog-eat-dog market, it first needs to retain what makes it so special. In its quest for constant improvement, it needs to hang on to its traditions. Second, its innovation efforts have to be built upon this foundation of tradition.

Wen Xiaoxi: As far as I know, Sichuan opera is indeed trying to innovate right now.

Da Meng: Right. For example, traditional Chinese musical instruments and Western instruments are used at the same time and some Western ways of singing are also employed. The state also supports the revival of Sichuan opera by, for example, building the Sichuan Opera Arts Center and organizing the "Sichuan opera meets campus" event, so that more people can understand and enjoy Sichuan opera.

词 语

huángdì emperor	**zhúgān** bamboo pole	**jiǎng** oar; paddle

bù kě sī yì 不可思议	inconceivable; unimaginable; unfathomable	hōng dòng 轰动	cause a sensation; create a stir
xiān 掀	stir up	gāo cháo 高潮	climax
qià dào hǎo chù 恰到好处	just right (for the purpose or occasion)	yǎn zòu 演奏	perform on a musical instrument
yuè qì 乐器	musical instrument	qì fēn 气氛	atmosphere; surrounding feeling
huó yuè 活跃	lively; excited	yī rán 依然	still; as before
fù xīng 复兴	revive; rejuvenate	jiǎng jiu 讲究	art; technique; sth. requiring careful study

xíng tou 行 头	actor's costume and paraphernalia
hú xū 胡 须	beard
huá lì 华 丽	magnificent; resplendent; gorgeous
xiān míng 鲜 明	(of color) bright; brilliant
liǎn pǔ 脸 谱	facial makeup or mask
háo mài 豪 迈	bold; heroic
zhèng zhí 正 直	honest; (person of) integrity
chén zhuó 沉 着	calm; composed
mén lián 门 帘	door curtain; portiere
mò shuǐ 墨 水	ink

xuē 靴	boots
chóng gāo 崇 高	noble
dǎ bàn 打 扮	dress up
qǐ fā 启 发	enlighten; stimulate
jī liè 激 烈	(of character) upright; unyielding
cán rěn 残 忍	cruel; ruthless
cū lǔ 粗 鲁	crude; boorish
jiān rèn 坚 韧	tenacious
duì yìng 对 应	corresponding; counterpart
chéng xiàn 呈 现	appear; emerge; present (a certain appearance)

lián xiǎng 联　想	associate with; make a mental connection; remind oneself of sth.
fēng tǔ rén qíng 风 土 人 情	local conditions and customs
píng jìng 平　静	calm
xiōng yǒng 汹　涌	surging; turbulent; raging
fù dān 负　担	burden
jí zhōng 集　中	focus; concentrate
chéng běn 成　本	cost
hào fèi 耗　费	consume; expend
mén piào 门　票	entrance ticket; admission ticket
jīng xīn 精　心	meticulous; elaborate

guī gēn dào dǐ 归 根 到 底	in the final analysis; after all; ultimately; in essence
fēi qín zǒu shòu 飞 禽 走 兽	the beasts of the field and the birds of the air
bō tāo 波　涛	great waves; billows
zǐ xì 仔　细	careful; attentive
zhē dǎng 遮　挡	cover
hū lüè 忽　略	ignore; overlook
píng mù 屏　幕	screen
zī yuán 资　源	resources
kāi zhī 开　支	expenses
cè huà 策　划	plan; program; design

chuán chéng 传 承	pass on (to future generations); continue a tradition; impart and inherit
duō yuán 多 元	pluralistic; multi-; poly-
zhòng suǒ zhōu zhī 众 所 周 知	as everyone knows
pǐn wèi 品 味	one's taste (In music, literature, fashion…)
míng zhì 明 智	sensible; wise
dé tiān dú hòu 得 天 独 厚	enjoy exceptional advantages; endowed by nature
xīn xīn xiàng róng 欣 欣 向 荣	thriving; flourishing
zài jiē zài lì 再 接 再 厉	make persistent efforts; continue to exert oneself

bì sè 闭 塞	inaccessible
chōng jī 冲 击	impact; affect
dà bù liǎo 大 不 了	(usu. used in the negative) (nothing) alarming; serious
fǎn sī 反 思	reflect; rethink; review
jí yú qiú chéng 急 于 求 成	anxious for quick results; impatient for results
yíng hé 迎 合	cater to; pander to
yōu shèng liè tài 优 胜 劣 汰	survival of the fittest
jīng yì qiú jīng 精 益 求 精	constantly improve

语言点

一、离合词
化妆

二、递进复句
不仅……还……

三、紧缩复句
一……就……

四、成语的使用

五、插入语
归根到底

思考

本课主要介绍了川剧的艺术特点，包括川剧的音乐、服装、化妆、舞台布置。现在，川剧的发展面临不少困难，三人谈论川剧的过去与未来、传承和发展，一直聊到了深夜。你对川剧的传承和创新有什么自己的建议吗？欢迎你积极提出自己的观点。

参考文献
[References]

[1] 孔子学院总部/国家汉办.国际汉语教学通用课程大纲 [M].北京：北京语言大学出版社，2014.

[2] 杜建华，王定欧.中国非物质文化遗产代表作丛书：川剧 [M].北京：文化艺术出版社，2012.

[3]《新世纪青少年艺术素质培养丛书》编委会.川剧入门与鉴赏 [M].北京：中国出版集团，世界图书出版公司，2012.

[4] 飞乐鸟.飞乐鸟的手绘旅行笔记：成都 [M].北京：人民邮电出版社，2016.

[5] 十品戏曲网.川剧《白蛇传》全剧剧本 [EB/OL].www.xqshipin.com/htmln/n/n381.html.

图书在版编目（CIP）数据

成都印象／西南财经大学 汉语国际推广成都基地著 —成都：西南财经
大学出版社，2019.7
（走进天府系列教材）
ISBN 987-7-5504-3776-0

Ⅰ．①成… Ⅱ．①西… Ⅲ．①汉语—对外汉语教学—教材②成都—
概况 Ⅳ．①H 195.4②K 927.11
中国版本图书馆 CIP 数据核字（2018）第 241717 号

走进天府系列教材：成都印象·看川剧
ZOUJIN TIANFU XILIE JIAOCAI:CHENGDU YINXIANG · KAN CHUANJU

西南财经大学 汉语国际推广成都基地 著

策　　划：王正好　何春梅
责任编辑：李　才
装帧设计：张艳洁
插　　画：辣点设计
责任印制：朱曼丽

出版发行	西南财经大学出版社（四川省成都市光华村街 55 号）
网　　址	http：//www.bookcj.com
电子邮件	bookcj@ foxmail.com
邮政编码	610074
电　　话	028-87353785
照　　排	上海辣点广告设计咨询有限公司
印　　刷	四川新财印务有限公司
成品尺寸	170mm×240mm
印　　张	46.5
字　　数	875 千字
版　　次	2019 年 7 月第 1 版
印　　次	2019 年 7 月第 1 次印刷
印　　数	1-2050 套
书　　号	ISBN 978-7-5504-3776-0
定　　价	198.00 元（套）